Growing
independence

To my children, Nicholas, Lara and Scarlett

ANNABEL KARMEL'S FAVOURITES

Growing independence

*Healthy home-made
recipes to encourage
self-feeding*

1 3 5 7 9 10 8 6 4 2

The Random House Group Limited Reg. No. 954009

A CIP catalogue record for this book is available from the British Library

ISBN: 978-009-195578-6

Printed in Hong Kong

Eddison•Sadd Editions
CREATIVE DIRECTOR Nick Eddison   INDEXER Dorothy Frame
SENIOR EDITOR Katie Golsby   DESIGNER Brazzle Atkins
PROOFREADER Nikky Twyman   ILLUSTRATIONS Nadine Wikenden
PRODUCTION Sarah Rooney

COVER PHOTOGRAPHY iStockphoto, Ruslan Dashinsky

Notes on the text:
- For fan-assisted ovens, reduce the temperature by 20°C.
- All black pepper is freshly ground.

Contents

Introduction

Around the age of nine months – a time of growing independence – you may notice that your baby is keen to feed himself. It's also not unusual, towards the end of the first year, for babies who started off as good eaters to become more fussy. This is because a baby's weight gain slows down dramatically at this stage, and this often means their appetite decreases. Your baby may well be mobile by now, and will therefore be far too busy moving around and showing off his new skills to want to be strapped into a chair and spoon fed!

In this book, you will find a broad selection of recipes to encourage your baby to feed himself, while ensuring that he continues to enjoy lots of new and interesting foods. Read on for more information about the foods to try between nine and twelve months and the developmental issues you may meet along the way.

Experimenting with food

Your baby's motor skills will be improving fast and it's likely that she will now be able to pick up objects between her thumb and fingers, rather than using a grabbing action. However, these skills won't yet be fine-tuned and will need a bit of practice. Give your baby finger foods to hold, and a small spoon or fork that she can grip easily. Put her food in a bowl with a suction pad and let her try scooping the food into her mouth. A lot of food will end up on the floor (I would advise putting a plastic splash mat under the chair), and she will probably use her hands to eat even the messiest foods, but the more she plays with the food, the sooner she will learn to feed herself.

Don't expect your baby to have good table manners at this age; exploring the feel of her food is all part of the learning process. Try to avoid wiping her face too much while she's eating. In my experience, babies who are allowed to play with their food tend to become the better eaters, and learn to feed themselves earlier, because they enjoy mealtimes. However, some behaviour, like throwing food, should be discouraged. If this occurs, simply remove the food and show your disapproval. Don't give your baby attention for bad behaviour.

You will need a lot of patience at mealtimes, as babies are very easily distracted at this stage, and it is a lot more fun to play than to eat. It is a good idea to eat something with your baby at mealtimes. Babies are great mimics, so try spooning food into your own mouth if your baby isn't interested in having any herself.

It's important to wash your baby's hands before she eats; however, there's no need to be obsessive about germs. You can wipe the tray on your baby's high chair with an anti-bacterial cleaner, but remember that your baby picks things up from the floor and puts them in her mouth all the time.

This stage is a risky time for swallowing objects other than food, and there is still a danger of choking on food, so make sure you keep an eye on your baby when she's eating.

Milk

Continue giving breast or formula milk as your baby's main drink. Cow's milk isn't suitable as a main drink for babies under one year of age, as it's low in essential vitamins and minerals such as iron. However, as the solid-food intake increases, milk becomes a less major part of the diet. Your baby should still be drinking about 500 ml (17 fl oz) of milk a day, as milk is still an important source of protein and calcium.

Aim to dispense with a baby bottle by the age of one year, instead giving milk in a beaker or cup. A beaker with a long, soft spout makes a good transition from a bottle. If it helps to settle your baby, you could continue to give a breast or bottle feed before you put him to bed.

Teething

Some babies get their first tooth around six months; others may hardly have any teeth by the time they are one year old. And, while some babies sail through the whole teething experience, it can be a pretty miserable time for others. Tell-tale teething signs include bright red cheeks, inflamed gums, a mild rash around the mouth, a mild fever and irritability. If you're concerned about your baby, you should check with your doctor or health visitor; don't just put it down to teething. Sore gums can often put babies off their food. Don't worry if your baby refuses to eat one day, as she will probably make up for it the next day.

Rubbing teething gel on your baby's gums can help relieve soreness and restore appetite. You can buy gel-filled teething rings that can be put in the fridge; these are easy for babies to hold and chew on. Cold finger foods are also effective. Try giving your baby chilled cucumber sticks to chew, or a banana that has been in the freezer for about 20 minutes. Homemade ice lollies are also great for soothing gums. You can make them using fruit juice, puréed fruit or yoghurt. Cold yoghurt or fromage frais can also help.

Babies often dribble while they're teething. Putting a little petroleum jelly around your baby's mouth can prevent the skin from becoming red and sore.

New foods
At this age, there aren't many foods that are unsuitable for your baby, so you can be quite adventurous with the foods you offer him. It's important not to give salt under the age of one year, but you can use herbs, spices and garlic to add some fantastic flavours, and these

have wonderful therapeutic properties. Try to vary the foods you give as much as possible, as this will lead to a more balanced diet.

Textures

If you haven't already done so, try varying the textures of your baby's food so that you're not only giving her soft foods. Not all babies take kindly to lumps, but it's important not to continue with smooth purées for too long, or your baby could develop a lazy attitude to chewing. It isn't essential to have teeth in order to chew, providing the food isn't too hard.

Mashing vegetables like potato, carrot and broccoli with a little butter, milk and cheese is a good way to introduce texture. Couscous is good, too, as are small pasta shapes.

Quantities

Just as when you first started weaning your baby, let his appetite be your guide as to how much to give him. He knows when he's had enough and when he is still hungry. Many of the recipes in this book can be frozen, so cook large batches and make lots of little portions. This way, if your baby is still hungry after one portion, you have more to give.

Vegetables

Now is a good time to try giving your baby any vegetables she hasn't yet tried. Green leafy vegetables can seem quite bitter to babies, but they're full of nutrients. Try mixing spinach, cabbage or kale with sweeter vegetables such as sweet potato or butternut squash.

You can make delicious vegetable sauces to go with pasta or couscous. If your baby isn't fond of lumps, blend the cooked vegetables to a very fine purée, as though you were making a soup. That way, she only has the lumps from the pasta or couscous to contend with.

When you start giving vegetables as finger food, make sure they're quite soft. Steaming is the best cooking method, as it preserves the most nutrients. Gradually reduce the cooking time as your baby gets older and more used to chewing.

Fruit

Berries are great for babies at this stage. Sieve the fruit if you're cooking it, or if it's frozen, to get rid of indigestible seeds. Make berry compotes (*see page 86*) or apple purée to make ice lollies or add to porridge.

Soft dried fruits are good for this stage, and are a good source of nutrients. However, don't give too much dried fruit, as it can be difficult to digest. Avoid apricots treated with sulphur dioxide, as they can trigger asthma attacks in susceptible babies.

Protein

It's vital to include a good variety of protein sources in your baby's diet. Between nine and twelve months, you can start to give chunky foods, such as mini meatballs, mini pies and Bolognese sauces. It is very important to include regular helpings of fish in your baby's diet. Oily fish, such as salmon, provide the best source of essential fatty acids, which are important for brain development.

Vegetarian proteins
If you have decided to raise your baby as a vegetarian, you must ensure that he has enough meat-free forms of protein, such as pulses, tofu and eggs. To ensure that iron is well absorbed, it's important to give vitamin C – for instance, a cup of orange juice – alongside iron-rich foods such as lentils or spinach. If your baby doesn't eat fish, it's important to provide an alternative source of omega 3, such as ground flaxseeds or flaxseed oil.

Carbohydrates
Toast soldiers, firm bread such as bagels, breadsticks and pitta all make good finger foods. Watch out for the level of sugar in rusks, as it is often quite high. Pasta is a great food for babies and you can make lots of delicious sauces from purées you may have stored in the freezer. Cooked pasta shapes also make good finger food.

Breakfast
Breakfast can become a little more interesting from nine months, as you can start to use a greater variety of grains. Make sure you check the ingredients when choosing cereal, as many children's cereals contain a huge amount of sugar. Mixing cereal with fruit makes a great breakfast.

Cheese is ideal for breakfast, as are eggs, both of which are great sources of calcium and protein. Make sure that eggs are well cooked – no runny yolks.

Recipe information

Each recipe is accompanied by helpful information on preparation and cooking times, how many portions the recipe makes and whether it's suitable for freezing. Preparation times and portion quantities should be used as a guide only, as these will vary.

On pages 92–3, you will find a meal planner to help you stay organized. This is intended to be used for guidance; you can, of course, use different recipes if you wish.

FINGER FOODS

Interestingly, many babies will happily chew on finger foods but refuse to take lumpy food from a spoon. Try putting some of the following suggestions on your baby's table and see what she makes of them.

Vegetables

At first, offer lightly steamed vegetables like sticks of carrot or parsnip and broccoli florets. Then move on to raw vegetables. It's often better to give a large piece of a vegetable or fruit that your baby can hold, rather than a small piece that he may struggle to pick up.

Fruit
Once your baby can manage soft fruits like pear, peach and banana, move on to harder fruits like peeled apple. Dried fruits like apricot or apple are very nutritious. You could tie a dried-apple ring to the high chair so that when your baby drops it you can easily retrieve it.

Breads
Try giving lots of different types of bread, like pitta bread, raisin bread, bagel, fingers of toast and naan bread. You could also try giving eggy bread or grilled cheese on toast.

Sandwiches

Make mini sandwiches with fillings such as: mashed banana; cream cheese with sugar-free strawberry jam; tuna mixed with a little mayonnaise and tomato ketchup; mashed sardines with a little tomato ketchup.

Cheese

Cheese is an excellent source of calcium. Give sticks or thin slices of Swiss cheese or Cheddar.

Meat and chicken

Try giving wafer-thin cooked meats rolled into a tube, or pieces of cooked chicken. Also try mini chicken balls (*see page 52*) or meatballs (*see page 62*).

Fish

You can make your own goujons of fish and coat them with crushed Rice Krispies and a little Parmesan cheese (*see page 41*). You can also make mini fish balls (*see page 39*).

Vegetables

Mashed potato and carrot with broccoli and cheese

Put the potatoes and carrots into a saucepan, cover with boiling water and cook for about 20 minutes, until tender. Put the broccoli in a steamer and cook for 7–8 minutes. Alternatively, steam the potato and carrot for 20 minutes, until tender. Add the broccoli about 7 minutes before the end of the cooking time.

Drain the potatoes and carrots, if necessary, and mash together with the broccoli, milk, butter and cheese.

🖊 6 MINUTES

📺 20 MINUTES

🍽 4 PORTIONS

❄ SUITABLE FOR FREEZING

300 g (11 oz) potatoes, peeled and cut into chunks
1 large carrot (125 g/4½ oz), peeled and sliced
75 g (3 oz) broccoli, washed and cut into florets
2 tablespoons milk
15 g (½ oz) unsalted butter
40 g (1½ oz) Cheddar cheese, grated

It is best to peel potatoes just before cooking; soaking them in water causes them to lose their vitamin C.

Mashed sweet potato with spinach and cheese

/ 5 MINUTES

⊡ 20 MINUTES

🥧 3 PORTIONS

❄ SUITABLE FOR FREEZING

1 small sweet potato (250 g/
   9 oz), peeled and chopped
a knob of unsalted butter
50 g (2 oz) fresh spinach,
   washed and roughly
   chopped
2 tablespoons cream cheese
25 g (1 oz) Cheddar cheese,
   grated

Put the sweet potato into a saucepan and cover with cold water. Bring to the boil and simmer for about 12 minutes, until tender. Drain and mash.

Melt the butter in a saucepan. Add the spinach and stir until wilted. Add the sweet potato, cream cheese and Cheddar. Stir over the heat until smooth.

Sweet potatoes are rich in vitamins C and E and betacarotene. It's a good idea to sometimes substitute them for ordinary potatoes.

Haricot bean, tomato and squash purée

Heat the oil in a frying pan and sauté the onion for 1 minute. Add the butternut squash and fry for 5 minutes, then stir in the garlic and fry for another minute. Add the beans, then the tomatoes, stock, sun-dried tomato paste and thyme. Bring to the boil, cover and simmer for 15 minutes.

Add the spinach and cook for 1 more minute, until the spinach is wilted.

Blend until smooth, then add the Parmesan cheese.

 15 MINUTES

 25 MINUTES

4 PORTIONS

SUITABLE FOR FREEZING

2 teaspoons sunflower oil
½ large onion (100 g/3½ oz), peeled and chopped
200 g (7 oz) butternut squash, peeled, deseeded and chopped
1 garlic clove, crushed
100 g (3½ oz) tinned haricot beans, drained and rinsed
200 g (7 oz) tinned chopped tomatoes
200 ml (7 fl oz) unsalted vegetable stock
15 g (½ oz) sun-dried tomato paste
1 teaspoon dried thyme
40 g (1½ oz) baby spinach leaves, washed
20 g (¾ oz) Parmesan cheese, grated

Tomato and sweet pepper sauce

/ 5 MINUTES

⬚ 15 MINUTES

⏲ 3–4 PORTIONS

❄ SUITABLE FOR FREEZING

50 g (2 oz) baby pasta shells
2 teaspoons olive oil
1 small onion (50 g/2 oz),
    peeled and chopped
25 g (1 oz) red pepper,
    washed, deseeded and
    chopped
½ garlic clove, crushed
400 g (14 oz) tinned
    chopped tomatoes
150 ml (¼ pint) water
1 tablespoon cream cheese
2 tablespoons apple juice

Cook the pasta according to the packet instructions.

Meanwhile, heat the oil in a saucepan. Add the onion and fry for 2 minutes. Add the red pepper and garlic and fry for another 2 minutes. Add the tomatoes and water, bring to the boil, then cover and simmer for 10 minutes.

Using an electric hand blender, blend the sauce until smooth. Add the cream cheese and apple juice and mix the sauce with the pasta.

Tomato sauce with carrots and basil

Put the carrots in a steamer over a pan of boiling water and cook for about 20 minutes or until tender.

Cook the pasta according to the packet instructions.

Meanwhile, melt the butter together with the oil, add the onion and sauté for 2 minutes, stirring occasionally. Add the courgette and sauté for 3 minutes, stirring occasionally. Add the tomato and basil, cover and cook for about 5 minutes, stirring occasionally until mushy. Stir in the cheese until melted.

When the carrots are cooked, blend together with the tomato sauce. Drain the pasta, stir into the sauce and serve.

To remove the skin from a tomato, cut a cross in the base using a sharp knife. Put in a bowl and cover with boiling water. Leave for 1 minute. Drain and rinse in cold water. The skin should peel off easily.

🖊 10 MINUTES

🗔 25 MINUTES

🍴 4 PORTIONS

❄ SUITABLE FOR FREEZING

2 medium carrots (200 g/ 7 oz), peeled and sliced
3 tablespoons tiny pasta shapes
15 g (½ oz) unsalted butter
1 teaspoon olive oil
½ small onion (30 g/1 oz), peeled and chopped
1 medium courgette (about 190 g/6½ oz), washed, topped and tailed, and sliced
4 ripe tomatoes, skinned (*see box, left*), deseeded and chopped
4–5 basil leaves, washed and shredded
50 g (2 oz) Cheddar cheese, grated

Risotto with butternut squash

⟋ 10 MINUTES

▭ 25 MINUTES

◷ 4 PORTIONS

✳ SUITABLE FOR FREEZING

25 g (1 oz) unsalted butter
1 small onion (50 g/2 oz),
   peeled and chopped
110 g (4 oz) basmati rice
450 ml (¾ pint) boiling
   water
150 g (5 oz) butternut
   squash, peeled, deseeded
   and chopped
225 g (8 oz) ripe tomatoes,
   skinned, deseeded and
   chopped
50 g (2 oz) Cheddar cheese,
   grated

Melt half the butter in a saucepan and sauté
the onion until softened. Stir in the rice until
well coated. Pour over the boiling water, cover
the pan and cook for 8 minutes over a high heat.
Stir in the butternut squash, reduce the heat and
simmer, covered, for about 12 minutes or until
the water has been absorbed.

Meanwhile, melt the remaining butter in a
small saucepan, add the tomatoes and sauté for
2–3 minutes. Stir in the cheese until melted, then
stir the tomato and cheese mixture into the
cooked rice.

*Butternut squash is rich in betacarotene, the plant
form of vitamin A, which helps protect against
cancer and will boost your baby's immune system.*

Vegetable couscous

Put the couscous into a bowl, pour over the stock or water and cover the bowl with clingfilm. Leave to absorb for 10 minutes.

Meanwhile, heat the oil in a saucepan. Add the onion, courgette and pepper, stir, then cover with a lid and sauté for 3–4 minutes. Stir in the garlic, then add the passata. Cover and simmer for 10 minutes.

Add the basil, then blend half of the mixture until smooth, using a hand blender. Mix with the chunky sauce and the couscous. If the consistency seems too thick for your baby, you could add a little extra water or stock.

🖊 10 MINUTES

▦ 15 MINUTES

🍳 3 PORTIONS

❄ SUITABLE FOR FREEZING

30 g (1 oz) couscous
100 ml (3½ fl oz) unsalted vegetable stock or water
1 teaspoon olive oil
½ medium red onion (75 g/ 3 oz), peeled and finely chopped
½ medium courgette (75 g/ 3 oz), washed, topped and tailed, and finely chopped
½ red pepper (50 g/2 oz), washed, deseeded and finely chopped
½ garlic clove, crushed
150 ml (¼ pint) passata
2 teaspoons chopped basil

Passata is simply sieved tomatoes, and you can buy it in any supermarket.

Herb omelette

⚗ 3 MINUTES

🍳 7 MINUTES

🍽 1–2 PORTIONS

❄ NOT SUITABLE FOR FREEZING

2 large eggs
2 tablespoons milk
1 tablespoon chopped basil
2 tablespoons chopped
    chives
30 g (1 oz) Cheddar cheese,
    grated
a knob of unsalted butter

In a small bowl, beat together the eggs, milk, herbs and Cheddar. Melt the butter in a small frying pan. Add the mixture and tilt the pan to cover the bottom, then cook until most of the mixture has set. Fold over one side, then turn the omelette over. Fry until cooked through and lightly golden on the outside. Leave to cool a little, then cut into bite-size pieces.

Eggs provide an excellent source of protein, zinc and vitamins A, D, E and B12. Most of the nutrients are concentrated in the yolk.

Fish

Tuna-melt toasties

⟋ 3 MINUTES

🖵 5–6 MINUTES

☕ 2 PORTIONS

❄ NOT SUITABLE FOR FREEZING

2 slices of white bread
unsalted butter for
    spreading
50 g (2 oz) tinned tuna,
    drained
1½ tablespoons mayonnaise
2 teaspoons chopped chives
¼ teaspoon Dijon mustard
½ tomato, washed and
    chopped
20 g (¾ oz) Gruyère cheese,
    grated

Toast the bread, then butter one side.

Preheat the grill. Mix together the tuna, mayonnaise, chives, mustard, tomato and half of the cheese. Spread on to the toast and sprinkle with the remaining cheese. Grill for 3–4 minutes, until lightly golden and bubbling on top.

Remove the crusts and cut into 8 squares. Serve warm.

Gruyère cheese has a slightly sweet taste that appeals to babies. Cheese is a good source of concentrated calories, protein and calcium.

Fillet of fish with carrot, tomato and cheese sauce

Steam the carrots for about 10 minutes or until tender.

Cook the pasta according to the packet instructions, then drain.

Meanwhile, place the fish in a microwave-proof dish, add the milk, dot with butter and cover, leaving an air vent. Microwave on high for about 1½ minutes. Alternatively, poach the fish in a saucepan of milk for a couple of minutes.

Melt 25 g (1 oz) butter in a saucepan and cook the tomato for 3 minutes, then stir in the cheese until melted.

Blend the fish together with the carrot and the sauce. Stir in the cooked pasta.

 6 MINUTES

15 MINUTES

3 PORTIONS

SUITABLE FOR FREEZING

2 medium carrots (150 g/ 5 oz), peeled and chopped
40 g (1½ oz) baby pasta shells
100 g (3½ oz) fillet of plaice, cod or pollack, skinned
1 tablespoon milk
25 g (1 oz) unsalted butter, plus extra to dot over the fish
3 medium tomatoes, skinned, deseeded and chopped
40 g (1½ oz) Cheddar cheese, grated

Decoration
3 cherry tomatoes, halved
6 short chive strips
3 small red-pepper triangles
6 basil leaves
a few green beans, cooked
a handful of rosemary leaves

Mini fish pie

Bring a pan of water to the boil, add the potatoes and simmer for about 20 minutes, until tender. Drain and mash with 25 g (1 oz) of butter and 1½ tablespoons of milk, until smooth.

Meanwhile, melt 15 g (½ oz) butter in a saucepan, add the onion and tomato and sauté until softened. Add the flour and stir over the heat for 30 seconds. Add the fish, parsley and bay leaf. Pour over the remaining milk and simmer for about 4 minutes, until the fish is cooked. Remove the bay leaf and stir in the cheese until melted.

Divide the fish mixture between 3 ramekin dishes (about 10 cm/4 in diameter) and top with the potato. Dot with a little butter and place under a preheated grill for a few minutes, until golden.

You could decorate each pie to make a cat's face. Cut the cherry tomatoes in half, and place a short strip of chive in the centre of each one to make the cat's eyes. Cut a triangle shape from the pepper for the nose. Make the mouth using short lengths of fine green beans and finish off with basil leaves for the ears and rosemary for the whiskers.

15 MINUTES

30 MINUTES

3 MINI FISH PIES

SUITABLE FOR FREEZING

375 g (13 oz) potatoes, peeled and cut into chunks

40 g (1½ oz) unsalted butter, plus extra for grilling

1½ tablespoons milk, plus 100 ml (3½ fl oz)

25 g (1 oz) onion, peeled and finely chopped

1 ripe tomato, skinned, deseeded and chopped

1 tablespoon flour

125 g (4½ oz) cod fillet, skinned and cubed

125 g (4½ oz) salmon fillet, skinned and cubed

1 teaspoon chopped parsley

1 bay leaf

40 g (1½ oz) Cheddar cheese, grated

Cod with leek, carrot and potatoes

📏 10 MINUTES

🍴 20 MINUTES

🍽 6 PORTIONS

❄ SUITABLE FOR FREEZING

a knob of unsalted butter
1 small stick celery, washed
  and finely chopped
1 small leek, peeled, washed
  and roughly chopped
1 small carrot (about 50 g/
  2 oz), peeled and finely
  chopped
100 g (3½ oz) potatoes,
  peeled and finely chopped
1 tablespoon plain flour
350 ml (12 fl oz) milk
15 g (½ oz) Parmesan cheese,
  grated
½ teaspoon Dijon mustard
150 g (5 oz) cod or haddock,
  skinned and cut into 2 cm
  (¾ in) cubes
1 tablespoon chopped chives
½ teaspoon lemon juice

Melt the butter in a saucepan. Add the celery, leek, carrot and potato and gently sauté for 3–4 minutes.

Sprinkle over the flour, then add the milk and stir until blended. Bring to the boil, stirring until the sauce has thickened. Cover and simmer for 8 minutes, until the vegetables are cooked.

Add the cheese, Dijon mustard and fish, and simmer for 5 minutes, until the fish is cooked through. Stir in the chives and lemon juice.

Fats from dairy produce, such as butter, cheese, yoghurt and milk, are fine for babies and they provide vitamins A and D. It is not good just to give fruit and vegetable purées, as they are low in calories.

Cod and pea pasta

/ 5 MINUTES

⟦ 10 MINUTES

🍪 4–6 PORTIONS

❄ SUITABLE FOR FREEZING

100 g (3½ oz) baby pasta
shells
50 g (2 oz) frozen peas
a knob of unsalted butter
½ medium onion (75 g/
3 oz), peeled and finely
chopped
1 teaspoon white wine
vinegar
100 ml (3½ fl oz) unsalted
fish stock
75 g (3 oz) cod fillet, skinned
and chopped
2 tablespoons cream cheese
1 teaspoon lemon juice
30 g (1 oz) Parmesan cheese,
grated

Cook the pasta following the packet instructions.
Add the peas 4 minutes before the end of the
cooking time, then drain.

Meanwhile, melt the butter in a saucepan.
Add the onion and gently cook for 5 minutes,
until soft. Add the white wine vinegar, stock and
cod, then bring to the boil. Simmer for 3 minutes,
until the cod is just cooked and starting to flake.
Add the cream cheese, lemon juice and pasta and
peas. Toss together over the heat, then add the
Parmesan.

Mini fish balls

Preheat the oven to 220°C/430°F/Gas 7.

Put all the ingredients except the breadcrumbs into a food processor. Whiz until roughly chopped. Add the breadcrumbs and whiz until combined. Shape into about 20 walnut-size balls.

Place the fish balls on a baking sheet lined with non-stick paper. Bake for 10–12 minutes, until cooked through and lightly golden.

Alternatively, you could fry the fish balls in a little sunflower oil.

✐ 25 MINUTES

▦ 10–12 MINUTES

🕤 20 FISH BALLS

❄ SUITABLE FOR FREEZING

125 g (4½ oz) salmon fillet, skinned and chopped
125 g (4½ oz) cod fillet, skinned and chopped
4 spring onions, washed and sliced
a pinch of lemon zest
2 teaspoons tomato ketchup
1 teaspoon sweet chilli sauce
40 g (1½ oz) Parmesan cheese, grated
1 tablespoon chopped dill
¼ teaspoon Dijon mustard
50 g (2 oz) white breadcrumbs

Fish should be cooked on the day it is bought to retain its freshness. Cod is high in protein and vitamin B12.

To freeze, lay the uncooked fish fingers on a baking sheet lined with clingfilm. Cover with clingfilm and freeze for 2 hours, until firm. Transfer to a freezer bag. Cook from frozen as described on the right (the cooking time is the same). Not suitable for reheating.

Krispie fish fingers with lemon-mayo dip

Cut the fish into little finger-size pieces. Cover and place in the fridge. Put the Rice Krispies, Parmesan and paprika in a food processor, and whiz to fine crumbs. Transfer to a plate and stir in a little black pepper. Spread out the flour on a separate plate.

Toss each of the fish pieces in the flour, dunk in the egg and roll in the Krispie crumbs until well coated. Place them on a clean plate. Cook them straight away or freeze as described in the box on the left.

To cook, heat the oil in a large frying pan and add the fish fingers. Fry for 1½–2 minutes on each side, until golden and cooked through. Transfer to a plate lined with kitchen paper to cool slightly before serving.

To make the dip, mix all the ingredients together in a small bowl. Serve with the fish fingers.

🖊 20 MINUTES

🍳 3–4 MINUTES

🕒 6–8 PORTIONS

❄ SUITABLE FOR FREEZING (UNCOOKED)

225 g (8 oz) skinless sole or plaice fillets
45 g (1½ oz) Rice Krispies
3 tablespoons Parmesan cheese, freshly grated
¼ teaspoon paprika
freshly ground black pepper
2 tablespoons plain flour
1 egg, beaten
2–3 tablespoons sunflower oil, for frying

For the dip
2 tablespoons mayonnaise
2 tablespoons Greek yoghurt
1 teaspoon fresh lemon juice

Salmon, cod and spinach risotto

🔪 10 MINUTES

🍳 12 MINUTES

🍽 6 PORTIONS

❄ NOT SUITABLE FOR FREEZING

150 g (5 oz) Basmati rice
a knob of unsalted butter
100 g (3½ oz) leek, washed, peeled and chopped
50 g (2 oz) fresh spinach, washed and chopped
100 g (3½ oz) salmon fillet, skinned
50 g (2 oz) cod fillet, skinned
50 ml (2 fl oz) milk
200 ml (7 fl oz) unsalted fish or chicken stock
1 teaspoon lemon juice
1 teaspoon chopped dill
40 g (1½ oz) Parmesan cheese, grated

Cook the rice according to the packet instructions, then drain.

Meanwhile, melt the butter in a saucepan. Add the leek and sauté for 5 minutes, until soft. Add the spinach and stir until wilted.

Place the salmon and cod in a microwave-proof bowl, add the milk and cover with clingfilm, piercing a few holes in the top. Cook in the microwave on High for 2 minutes, until cooked through. Alternatively, poach the fish in 100 ml (3½ fl oz) milk until just tender. Drain and reserve 50 ml (2 fl oz) of the milk. Flake the fish, checking for any remaining bones.

Add the stock to the leek and spinach and bring to the boil. Stir for 1 minute, then add the flaked fish and milk. Remove from the heat and add the lemon juice, dill and Parmesan, then stir in the rice.

Cod balls

Put all the ingredients except the oil into a food processor and whiz until combined. Shape into about 18 walnut-size balls.

Heat the oil in a frying pan and fry the cod balls for 8–10 minutes, turning regularly, until lightly golden and cooked through. Serve warm with tomato ketchup.

✏ 15 MINUTES

🗔 8–10 MINUTES

🍪 18 COD BALLS

❄ SUITABLE FOR FREEZING

50 g (2 oz) white
  breadcrumbs
200 g (7 oz) cod fillet,
  skinned
30 g (1 oz) mature Cheddar
  cheese, grated
6 spring onions, washed
  and sliced
2 teaspoons sweet chilli
  sauce
1 teaspoon tomato ketchup
1 teaspoon soy sauce
  (optional)
a little sunflower oil
  for frying

Fish is an excellent low-fat source of protein. It is important to encourage a liking for fish early on.

Chicken

Chunky chicken purée

Heat the oil in a saucepan. Add the leek and carrot and fry for 2 minutes. Add the flour, then blend in the stock, cover and simmer for 5 minutes. Add the chicken, broccoli and milk and simmer for another 5 minutes, until the vegetables are soft and the chicken is cooked through.

Blend half of the mixture using an electric hand blender. Mix in with the rest of the mixture and add the Parmesan. Stir until smooth.

🖊 10 MINUTES

🔲 15 MINUTES

🍪 3 PORTIONS

❄ SUITABLE FOR FREEZING

1 teaspoon olive oil
50 g (2 oz) leek, washed, peeled and chopped
1 medium carrot (75 g/3 oz), peeled and chopped
1 teaspoon plain flour
200 ml (7 fl oz) unsalted chicken stock
100 g (3½ oz) chicken breast fillet, finely chopped
50 g (2 oz) tiny broccoli florets, washed
150 ml (¼ pint) milk
15 g (½ oz) Parmesan cheese, grated

Chicken is a growth food, as it is packed with protein and vitamin B12, which isn't found in plant foods. Chicken also naturally contains fat, which is used for energy and growth.

Chicken with carrot and apple

/ 12 MINUTES

🗔 30 MINUTES

🍪 6 PORTIONS

❄ SUITABLE FOR FREEZING

1 tablespoon sunflower oil
60 g (2 oz) leek, peeled,
    washed and finely
    chopped
25 g (1 oz) celery, washed
    and chopped
1 medium carrot (75 g/
    3 oz), peeled and chopped
1 small garlic clove, crushed
100 g (3½ oz) chicken,
    chopped
250 g (9 oz) sweet potato,
    peeled and chopped
75 g (3 oz) apple, peeled,
    cored and chopped
a sprig of thyme
250 ml (8 fl oz) unsalted
    chicken stock or boiling
    water

Heat the oil in a saucepan and sauté the leek for 2 minutes, then add the celery and carrot and cook for another 5 minutes. Add the garlic, cook for 1 minute, then stir in the chicken. Sauté for 2–3 minutes, or until the chicken is sealed. Add the sweet potato, apple and thyme and pour over the stock or boiling water. Cover and simmer over a low heat for 20 minutes. Remove the sprig of thyme and blitz to a purée.

Chicken contains the antioxidant selenium, which helps to protect us from heart disease and some cancers.

Cherub's couscous

Bring the chicken stock to the boil and pour over the couscous. Stir with a fork and set aside for 10 minutes, by which time it will have absorbed the stock.

Meanwhile, melt the butter in a saucepan and sauté the onion for 2 minutes. Add the courgettes and sauté for about 4 minutes, then add the tomatoes and cook for 1 minute.

Fluff up the couscous with a fork and mix in the courgette and tomato mixture, together with the chicken.

🖊 7 MINUTES

⬛ 8 MINUTES

🍽 4 PORTIONS

❄ NOT SUITABLE FOR FREEZING

250 ml (8 fl oz) unsalted
   chicken stock
100 g (3½ oz) couscous
15 g (½ oz) unsalted butter
½ small onion (25 g/1 oz),
   peeled and chopped
50 g (2 oz) courgettes,
   washed, topped and tailed
   and chopped
2 tomatoes, skinned,
   deseeded and chopped
50 g (2 oz) cooked chicken,
   chopped

Couscous is a form of grain made from wheat and is popular in Middle Eastern cuisine. It's quite high in minerals and vitamins, and has a mild taste and wonderful soft texture. It is also very quick and easy to prepare.

Chicken and vegetable pies

🔪 12 MINUTES

🗓 20 MINUTES

🍳 3 PORTIONS

❄️ SUITABLE FOR FREEZING

150 g (5 oz) white potatoes,
  peeled and cut into chunks
100 g (3½ oz) sweet potatoes,
  peeled and chopped
15 g (½ oz) unsalted butter,
  plus extra for mashing
250 ml (8 fl oz) milk, plus
  extra for mashing
75 g (3 oz) leek, washed,
  peeled and finely chopped
½ small carrot (30 g/1 oz),
  peeled and grated
1 teaspoon white wine
  vinegar
100 g (3½ oz) chicken breast
  fillet, finely chopped
2 tablespoons plain flour
¼ teaspoon chopped thyme
a little Cheddar cheese,
  grated

First, make the potato topping. Bring a saucepan
of water to the boil and add the potato and
sweet potato. Simmer for 12–15 minutes or until
tender. Drain, then mash. Add a small knob of
butter and 2 tablespoons of milk, and stir until
smooth.

Melt the butter in a frying pan, add the leek
and carrot and sauté for 5 minutes. Add the
white wine vinegar and chicken and stir. Add
the flour, then blend in the milk and stir until
thickened. Stir in the thyme and simmer for
2 minutes, until the chicken is cooked through.

Preheat the grill. Spoon the chicken mixture
into three ramekins. Top with the mashed potato
and sprinkle with cheese.
Grill for 5 minutes, until
lightly golden and bubbling.

Parmesan chicken fingers

Cut the chicken breast in half horizontally through the centre. Put the two pieces between two sheets of clingfilm and beat with a mallet or rolling pin until they are no more than 5 mm ($\frac{1}{4}$ in) thick. Remove the clingfilm and cut the chicken into thin strips, about 5 cm (2 in) long.

Beat the egg white with a little pepper, until frothy. Spread out the Parmesan on a large plate. Dip the chicken strips in the egg white and roll in the Parmesan to coat.

Preheat the grill to High and line a grill pan with foil. Grill the chicken fingers for 2–3 minutes, until the cheese is golden. Turn over and cook for a further 2–3 minutes, until the chicken has cooked through. Cool slightly before serving.

This is a good recipe for children with a wheat or gluten allergy.

🔪 15 MINUTES

🍳 6 MINUTES

🕐 3–4 PORTIONS

❄ SUITABLE FOR FREEZING (UNCOOKED)

1 boneless, skinless chicken breast (about 125 g/4½ oz)
1 egg white
freshly ground black pepper
50 g (2 oz) Parmesan cheese, grated

To freeze, lay the uncooked chicken fingers on a baking sheet lined with clingfilm. Cover with clingfilm and freeze until firm. Transfer the chicken fingers to a freezer bag and return to the freezer until needed. Cook from frozen, adding 1 minute to the cooking time. These aren't suitable for reheating, but are good cold.

Mini chicken balls

🔪 20 MINUTES

🔲 8–10 MINUTES

🍳 20 CHICKEN BALLS

❄️ SUITABLE FOR FREEZING

250 g (9 oz) minced chicken
3 spring onions, washed
  and chopped
1 small carrot (40 g/1½ oz),
  peeled and finely grated
30 g (1 oz) apple, peeled,
  cored and grated
1 tablespoon chopped basil
40 g (1½ oz) Parmesan
  cheese, grated
2 teaspoons sweet chilli
  sauce
2 teaspoons soy sauce
50 g (2 oz) white
  breadcrumbs
1 tablespoon plain flour,
  plus extra for coating
a little sunflower oil for
  frying

Put all the ingredients except the oil into a large mixing bowl and combine well. Shape into 20 walnut-size balls. Coat in a little extra flour.

Heat a little oil in a frying pan and fry the chicken balls for 8–10 minutes, turning regularly, until lightly golden and cooked through.

For something a little different, you could substitute the chicken for minced turkey.

Fruity chicken curry with pasta

Cook the pasta following the packet instructions, then drain.

Heat the oil in a frying pan. Add the onion and ginger and sauté for 5 minutes. Add the korma paste, then the stock and coconut milk. Add the apricots and squash, then bring to the boil and simmer, covered, for 10 minutes, until the squash is tender. Whiz using a hand blender until smooth.

Fry the chicken for 3–4 minutes, then add the sauce. Finally, stir in the drained pasta.

✎ 8 MINUTES

▦ 20 MINUTES

🍳 4 PORTIONS

❄ SUITABLE FOR FREEZING

60 g (2 oz) baby pasta shells
2 teaspoons sunflower oil
50 g (2 oz) onion, peeled and finely chopped
¼ teaspoon grated ginger
2 teaspoons korma paste
150 ml (¼ pint) unsalted chicken stock
100 ml (3½ fl oz) coconut milk
15 g (½ oz) dried apricots, roughly chopped
50 g (2 oz) butternut squash, peeled, deseeded and finely chopped
75 g (3 oz) chicken breast fillet, chopped into small pieces

Korma paste has a slightly sweet flavour, which is ideal for younger palates.

Chicken Bolognese

📏 6 MINUTES

🍲 25 MINUTES

🍽 2 PORTIONS

❄ SUITABLE FOR FREEZING

25 g (1 oz) spaghetti
1 tablespoon olive oil
1 small onion (about 50 g/
  2 oz), peeled and chopped
1 garlic clove, crushed
1 small carrot (50 g/2 oz),
  peeled and grated
150 g (5 oz) minced chicken
  or turkey
½ teaspoon fresh thyme
  leaves or a pinch of dried
  thyme
150 ml (¼ pint) passata
150 ml (¼ pint) unsalted
  chicken stock

Cook the spaghetti according to the packet instructions.

Meanwhile, heat the oil in a saucepan, add the onion and garlic and sauté for 3 minutes. Add the carrots and continue to cook for 3 minutes. Tip in the mince and cook, stirring occasionally, for about 3 minutes, until browned. Add the thyme, passata and stock, bring to the boil, then cover and simmer for 15 minutes.

Drain the spaghetti and chop into small pieces.

Using a hand blender, whiz the Bolognese sauce for a few seconds to make a smoother texture, then stir in the chopped spaghetti.

It's good to use minced or chopped chicken thigh, as the dark meat of the chicken is richer in iron than the breast.

Meat

Tender casserole of lamb

🖊 10 MINUTES

🍳 60 MINUTES

🍪 6 PORTIONS

❄ SUITABLE FOR FREEZING

2 lamb cutlets (about 160 g/
5½ oz in total)
½ small onion (about 40 g/
1½ oz), peeled and chopped
200 g (7 oz) potatoes, peeled
and chopped
1 large carrot (110 g/4 oz),
peeled and sliced
2 tomatoes, skinned,
deseeded and chopped
125 ml (4 fl oz) unsalted
chicken stock

Preheat the oven to 180°C/350°F/Gas 4. Put the lamb cutlets, vegetables and stock into a small casserole, cover with a lid and cook in the oven for about 1 hour, until the lamb is tender. Chop into small pieces, or purée for younger babies.

Lamb is high in protein, which is essential for growing, and a good source of iron, zinc and B vitamins. Lamb tends to be more fatty than beef, so trim off any excess fat.

Lamb, aubergine and sweet potato pies

✎ 10 MINUTES

▦ 45–55 MINUTES

◷ 4 PORTIONS

❋ SUITABLE FOR FREEZING

Heat the oil in a frying pan. Add the onion and fry for 2 minutes. Add the mince and brown over the heat, then drain any fat. Stir in the garlic and aubergine, then add the flour, cinnamon, oregano, tinned tomatoes and sun-dried tomato paste. Bring to the boil, then cover and simmer for 30–40 minutes, until the aubergine is tender.

Meanwhile, bring a saucepan of water to the boil. Put in the white potato and sweet potato, cover and simmer for 12–15 minutes, or until tender. Drain the water from the potatoes and mash with a little butter and milk.

Add the Parmesan to the mince and spoon the mixture into 4 ramekins. Spoon the mashed potato on top.

Place the pies under a preheated grill for 5 minutes, until bubbling and lightly golden.

1 tablespoon sunflower oil
1 medium red onion (about 140 g/5 oz), peeled and chopped
200 g (7 oz) minced lamb
1 garlic clove, crushed
75 g (3 oz) aubergine, washed and chopped
1 teaspoon plain flour
¼ teaspoon ground cinnamon
½ teaspoon dried oregano
400 g (14 oz) tinned chopped tomatoes
1 teaspoon sun-dried tomato paste
200 g (7 oz) white potato, peeled and chopped
150 g (5 oz) sweet potato, peeled and chopped
a little unsalted butter
a little milk
2 tablespoons Parmesan cheese, grated

Mini shepherd's pie

Put the potato and carrot into a saucepan, just cover with boiling water, and cook for about 20 minutes, until tender.

Meanwhile, heat the vegetable oil in a saucepan and sauté the onion until softened. Add the minced meat and sauté, stirring occasionally, until browned. Add the tomato and ketchup and pour over the stock. Cover, bring to the boil and simmer for about 20 minutes.

When the potatoes and carrots are cooked, drain and return to the pan, together with the butter and milk, and mash with a potato masher or potato ricer until smooth. Mix with the mince.

🖊 10 MINUTES

📅 30 MINUTES

☕ 2 PORTIONS

❄ SUITABLE FOR FREEZING

300 g (11 oz) potatoes, peeled and cut into chunks
1 medium carrot (100 g/ 3½ oz), peeled and sliced
1 tablespoon vegetable oil
½ small onion (25 g/1 oz), peeled and chopped
100 g (3½ oz) lean minced beef or lamb
1 tomato, skinned, deseeded and chopped
1 teaspoon tomato ketchup
150 ml (¼ pint) unsalted chicken stock
15 g (½ oz) unsalted butter
2 tablespoons milk

To add some fun to this meal, you could make mini shepherd's pies and give them faces made from vegetables.

Mini meatballs

🖊 15 MINUTES

📟 18–20 MINUTES

🍳 24 MEATBALLS

❄ SUITABLE FOR FREEZING

85 g (3 oz) white
breadcrumbs
250 g (9 oz) minced beef
½ large onion (100 g/3½ oz),
peeled and chopped
½ apple, peeled, cored and
grated
1 garlic clove, crushed
30 g (1 oz) Parmesan cheese,
grated
1 teaspoon chopped thyme
2 teaspoons Worcestershire
sauce
1 teaspoon tomato purée
1 egg yolk
freshly ground black pepper

Preheat the oven to 220°C/430°F/Gas 7. Put all
the ingredients into a food processor and whiz
until chopped. Shape into 24 walnut-size balls.

Place the meatballs on a large baking sheet
and bake in the oven for 18–20 minutes, turning
halfway through the cooking time. Alternatively,
fry them in sunflower oil, turning regularly, until
cooked through.

*These tasty meatballs make great finger food. You
could serve them with steamed vegetables, such as
carrot sticks or broccoli or cauliflower florets.*

Meatballs with spaghetti and tomato sauce

🥄 25 MINUTES

🔲 30 MINUTES

🍳 8 PORTIONS

❄️ SUITABLE FOR FREEZING

To make the meatballs, first soak the breadcrumbs in the milk for about 5 minutes. Heat 1 tablespoon of the oil, add the onion and sauté for about 3 minutes, until softened. Transfer to a food processor with the rest of the ingredients, except the remaining oil and spaghetti. Briefly blend until mixed, and then shape into about 16 balls using floured hands. If you have time, chill them in the fridge for a while, but it isn't essential.

Cook the spaghetti according to the packet instructions.

Meanwhile, heat 2 tablespoons of vegetable oil in a large frying pan and fry the meatballs over a high setting to seal, then reduce the heat and cook for 5–6 minutes, turning occasionally.

To make the sauce, heat the olive oil in a saucepan, add the onion and garlic and sauté for 5–6 minutes. Stir in the passata and basil and season to taste. Simmer for 5–6 minutes, then add the meatballs and leave the sauce to simmer for a few minutes longer. Serve with the spaghetti.

60 g (2 oz) white breadcrumbs
2 tablespoons milk
3 tablespoons vegetable oil
1 small onion (50 g/2 oz), peeled and finely chopped
½ apple, peeled, cored and grated
225 g (8 oz) minced beef
1 tablespoon chopped parsley
2 tablespoons Parmesan cheese, grated
½ egg, lightly beaten
a little Worcestershire sauce
freshly ground black pepper
plain flour
200 g (7 oz) spaghetti

Tomato sauce
2 tablespoons olive oil
1 onion, peeled and chopped
1 garlic clove, crushed
500 ml (17 fl oz) passata
a few basil leaves, chopped
freshly ground black pepper

Cherub's chilli con carne

/ 5 MINUTES

[ ] 40–50 MINUTES

6 PORTIONS

SUITABLE FOR FREEZING

1 teaspoon sunflower oil
½ large onion (about
    100 g/3½ oz), peeled
    and chopped
200 g (7 oz) minced beef
½ red pepper (50 g/2 oz),
    washed, deseeded and
    chopped
1 garlic clove, crushed
¼ teaspoon ground
    cinnamon
¼ teaspoon ground cumin
¼ teaspoon ground
    coriander
300 ml (½ pint) passata
100 ml (3½ fl oz) water
1 teaspoon sun-dried
    tomato paste
75 g (3 oz) haricot beans

Heat the oil in a saucepan. Add the onion and fry for 2 minutes. Add the mince and brown over the heat. Add the pepper, garlic and spices, then mix in the passata, water, sun-dried tomato paste and beans. Bring to the boil, cover and simmer for 30–40 minutes, until cooked through. Serve with rice.

Pasta

Courgette, tomato and basil pasta

Cook the pasta following the packet instructions. Reserve 100 ml (3½ fl oz) of the cooking water before draining.

Melt the butter in a saucepan. Add the onion and courgette and fry for 5–8 minutes, until soft. Add the garlic and fry for 30 seconds. Add the tomato, sun-dried tomato paste and reserved water. Add the pasta and basil and toss together. Serve and sprinkle the Cheddar on top.

✎ 8 MINUTES

▦ 7–10 MINUTES

🕤 4–6 PORTIONS

❄ SUITABLE FOR FREEZING

75 g (3 oz) baby pasta shells
20 g (¾ oz) unsalted butter
½ medium onion (75 g/3 oz), peeled and finely chopped
½ medium courgette (100 g/ 3½ oz), washed, topped and tailed, and finely chopped
1 garlic clove, crushed
1 tomato, washed, deseeded and chopped
1 tablespoon sun-dried tomato paste
2 tablespoons chopped basil
30 g (1 oz) mature Cheddar cheese, grated

Pasta is a great energy food, packed with B vitamins and complex carbohydrates.

Pasta risotto

✐ 5 MINUTES

🖵 12 MINUTES

🍴 4 PORTIONS

❄ SUITABLE FOR FREEZING

75 g (3 oz) orzo or other
small pasta shapes
1 small carrot (50 g/2 oz),
peeled and chopped
50 g (2 oz) courgettes,
washed, topped and
tailed, and chopped
50 g (2 oz) broccoli florets,
washed and chopped
25 g (1 oz) unsalted butter
25 g (1 oz) Cheddar or
Parmesan cheese, grated

Put the pasta in a saucepan, together with the
carrot. Cover generously with boiling water
and cook for 5 minutes. Add the courgettes
and broccoli and continue to cook for about
7 minutes.

Melt the butter in a saucepan, stir in the
drained pasta and vegetables, then add the
butter and cheese and toss until melted.

*Orzo are tiny pasta shapes that look like rice.
If you can't find them, you could use any other
small pasta shapes instead.*

Stars with tomatoes and pesto

/ 3 MINUTES

▢ 15 MINUTES

🍳 4 PORTIONS

❄ SUITABLE FOR FREEZING

100 g (3½ oz) baby pasta stars
a knob of unsalted butter
2 tomatoes, washed,
    deseeded and finely
    chopped
2 tablespoons fresh pesto
30 g (1 oz) Cheddar cheese,
    grated

Cook the pasta following the packet instructions,
then drain.

Melt the butter in a saucepan. Add the pasta
and tomatoes and stir for 2 minutes. Add the
pesto and cheese and stir for another 2 minutes.

Avocado, pea and chive pasta

/ 3 MINUTES

▢ 11 MINUTES

🍳 1 PORTION

❄ NOT SUITABLE FOR FREEZING

25 g (1 oz) baby pasta shells
50 g (2 oz) frozen peas
a little unsalted chicken
    stock, crumbled
1 tablespoon cream cheese
20 g (¾ oz) Parmesan
    cheese, grated
¼ avocado, peeled, stoned
    and finely chopped
2 teaspoons chopped chives

Cook the pasta following the packet instructions.
Add the peas 5 minutes before the end of the
cooking time. Reserve 3 tablespoons of pasta
water before draining.

Put the water in a saucepan and add the
crumbled stock. Add the pasta and peas, cream
cheese, Parmesan, avocado and chives. Stir over
the heat for 1 minute.

Broccoli and cauliflower pasta

Melt the butter in a saucepan. Add the onion and fry for 2 minutes. Stir in the broccoli and cauliflower, sprinkle over the flour, then blend in the milk. Cover and simmer for 10 minutes.

Meanwhile, cook the pasta following the packet instructions.

Blend the mixture using an electric hand blender until smooth, then stir in the cheese.

Drain the pasta, then add to the sauce. Add a few tablespoons of water if the sauce is a little too thick.

🕐 5 MINUTES

🍳 15 MINUTES

🕐 2–3 PORTIONS

❄ SUITABLE FOR FREEZING

a knob of unsalted butter
½ small onion (25 g/1 oz), peeled and finely chopped
40 g (1½ oz) small broccoli florets
100 g (3½ oz) small cauliflower florets
2 teaspoons plain flour
250 ml (8 fl oz) milk
50 g (2 oz) baby pasta shells
30 g (1 oz) mature Cheddar cheese, grated

Pasta with tomato and mascarpone sauce

🖊 10 MINUTES

📅 20 MINUTES

🍪 4 PORTIONS

❄ SUITABLE FOR FREEZING

Cook the pasta following the packet instructions, then drain.

Meanwhile, heat the oil in a saucepan and sauté the onion, carrot, courgette and celery for 5 minutes. Add the garlic and sauté for 1 minute. Add the mushrooms and sauté for 2 minutes. Stir in the passata or tinned tomatoes with the apple juice, cover and simmer for 10 minutes, stirring occasionally.

Remove the tomato sauce from the heat, add the basil (if using) and blend in a food processor. Return to the pan and stir in the mascarpone and Parmesan. Stir the sauce into the pasta.

To make a creamy tomato and chicken Bolognese sauce, simply add 75 g (3 oz) chopped, cooked chicken breast at the same time as the mushrooms.

60 g (2 oz) baby pasta shells
1 tablespoon olive oil
1 red onion (about 140 g/5 oz), peeled and chopped
½ small carrot (30 g/1 oz), peeled and chopped
30 g (1 oz) courgette, washed, topped and tailed, and chopped
15 g (½ oz) celery, washed and chopped
1 garlic clove, crushed
50 g (2 oz) mushrooms, washed and chopped
400 ml (14 fl oz) passata or 400 g (14 oz) tinned chopped tomatoes
2 tablespoons apple juice
2 tablespoons torn basil leaves (optional)
3 tablespoons mascarpone cheese
3 tablespoons grated Parmesan cheese

Mushroom and spinach pasta

✎ 8 MINUTES

⊞ 18 MINUTES

🍳 4 PORTIONS

❄ SUITABLE FOR FREEZING

60 g (2 oz) baby pasta shells
10 g (¼ oz) unsalted butter
1 small onion (50 g/2 oz),
   peeled and finely chopped
50 g (2 oz) chestnut
   mushrooms, washed and
   finely chopped
1 garlic clove, crushed
10 g (¼ oz) plain flour
250 ml (8 fl oz) milk
¼ teaspoon chopped thyme
30 g (1 oz) Parmesan cheese,
   grated
30 g (1 oz) baby spinach,
   washed and finely
   chopped

Cook the pasta following the packet instructions, then drain.

Meanwhile, melt the butter in a saucepan, add the onion, cover and sauté for 8 minutes or until softened. Add the mushrooms and fry for 3 minutes. Add the garlic and fry for 2 minutes. Add the flour, then add the milk, stirring until thickened. Add the thyme, Parmesan and spinach and stir until the spinach is wilted. Stir in the pasta.

Spinach is rich in chlorophyll, the green pigment found in plants which helps to prevent and treat anaemia.

Bolognese with vegetables

/ 10 MINUTES

▯ 30 MINUTES

🍪 3 PORTIONS

❄ SUITABLE FOR FREEZING

1 tablespoon light olive oil
2 shallots (about 50 g/2 oz),
    peeled and chopped
1 small carrot (50 g/2 oz),
    peeled and chopped
20 g (³/₄ oz) celery, washed
    and chopped
1 small garlic clove, crushed
50 g (2 oz) butternut
    squash, peeled, deseeded
    and chopped
200 g (7 oz) tinned chopped
    tomatoes
150 g (5 oz) lean minced beef
1 teaspoon tomato purée
100 ml (3½ fl oz) unsalted
    beef or chicken stock, or
    water
1 teaspoon fresh thyme
    leaves
50 g (2 oz) organic baby
    pasta stars

Heat the oil in a saucepan and gently sauté the shallots, carrot and celery for 7–8 minutes, until softened. Add the garlic and cook for 30 seconds. Add the butternut squash and tomatoes and cook for 5 minutes.

Meanwhile, brown the mince in a frying pan with no oil.

Transfer the vegetables to a food processor and blend until smooth. Return them to the pan and add the tomato purée, stock, thyme and mince. Cover and simmer for 12–15 minutes, adding a little more stock if necessary.

Meanwhile, cook the pasta according to the packet instructions. Drain, then toss with the sauce.

You could mix this Bolognese with some potato mashed with a little butter and milk, and maybe a little grated Cheddar cheese. You could also use minced turkey or chicken instead of beef.

Pasta shells with salmon and broccoli

To cook the salmon, place it in a saucepan with a little of the stock and poach over a low heat for 3–4 minutes, or until it flakes easily with a fork. Alternatively, place in a microwave-proof dish with 2 tablespoons of stock and cook in the microwave on High for about 2 minutes.

Meanwhile, cook the pasta according to the packet instructions, then drain.

To make the sauce, melt the butter in a saucepan, then add the onion and sauté for 3–4 minutes, until just soft. Add the flour and mix together, then blend in the remaining stock and the milk. Bring to the boil. Add the broccoli and simmer, covered, for 5–6 minutes, until soft.

Whiz in a food processor until smooth. Stir in the crème fraîche, Parmesan, lemon juice, herbs and cooked salmon. Return to the pan and simmer for 2 minutes. Serve with the pasta.

✎ 8 MINUTES
⊞ 15–18 MINUTES
🍽 4 PORTIONS
❄ SUITABLE FOR FREEZING

50 g (2 oz) salmon fillet
150 ml (¼ pint) unsalted vegetable or chicken stock
40 g (1½ oz) baby pasta shells
a knob of unsalted butter
½ small onion (about 40 g/ 1½ oz), peeled and finely chopped
2 teaspoons plain flour
100 ml (3½ fl oz) milk
50 g (2 oz) broccoli, washed and roughly chopped
3 tablespoons crème fraîche
3 tablespoons grated Parmesan cheese
1 teaspoon lemon juice
½ teaspoon chopped dill
½ teaspoon chopped chives

Creamy chicken and basil pasta

🔪 7 MINUTES

🍳 15 MINUTES

🍽 1 PORTION

❄ SUITABLE FOR FREEZING

25 g (1 oz) baby pasta shells
1 teaspoon olive oil
½ small onion (20 g/¾ oz),
  peeled and finely chopped
1 small tomato, deseeded
  and finely chopped
30 g (1 oz) chicken breast
  fillet, finely chopped
4 tablespoons unsalted
  chicken stock
1 teaspoon chopped basil
15 g (½ oz) Parmesan
  cheese, grated
1 tablespoon single cream

Cook the pasta in boiling water according to the packet instructions, then drain.

Meanwhile, heat the oil and fry the onion for 3 minutes. Add the tomato and fry for 1 minute. Add the chicken and fry, turning regularly, until cooked through. Then add the stock, pasta, basil, Parmesan and cream, and stir until heated through.

Tomatoes are rich in potassium, which is important for healthy blood and helps to counteract the negative effect of salt.

Fruit

Fruity breakfast muesli

Put the porridge oats and wheatgerm, if using, into a bowl, and pour over the apple and mango juice. Leave to soak for 1 hour or overnight. Before serving, stir in the apple and grapes.

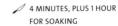

🖊 4 MINUTES, PLUS 1 HOUR
FOR SOAKING

🕐 1–2 PORTIONS

❄ NOT SUITABLE FOR FREEZING

20 g (¾ oz) porridge oats
½ tablespoon wheatgerm (optional)
75 ml (2½ fl oz) apple and mango juice (or apple juice)
½ small apple, peeled, cored and grated
4 grapes, peeled, deseeded and chopped

Baby muesli

Mix together the oats, apricots, raisins and ground almonds in the plastic bowl of an electric hand blender. Pour over the juice and leave to soak for 5 minutes. When softened, blend to make a finer texture, then stir in the grated apple.

🖊 8 MINUTES

🕐 1 PORTION

❄ NOT SUITABLE FOR FREEZING

2 tablespoons porridge oats
1 tablespoon finely chopped dried apricots
½ tablespoon raisins
1 tablespoon ground almonds
4 tablespoons pure apple, orange or pineapple juice
½ small dessert apple, peeled and grated

Mini banana bran muffins

✎ 10 MINUTES

▦ 12 MINUTES

🍪 24 MUFFINS

❄ SUITABLE FOR FREEZING

50 g (2 oz) Bran Flakes
75 ml (2½ fl oz) warm milk
1 medium banana, peeled
   and mashed
1 egg yolk
50 ml (2 fl oz) sunflower oil
50 g (2 oz) raisins
60 g (2 oz) soft light brown
   sugar
60 g (2 oz) wholemeal plain
   flour
½ teaspoon bicarbonate
   of soda
½ teaspoon baking powder
½ teaspoon ground
   cinnamon
¼ teaspoon ground ginger

Preheat the oven to 180°C/350°F/Gas 4. Line
two 12-hole mini-muffin tins with paper cases.

Mix together the Bran Flakes, milk and banana
and leave to stand for 5 minutes. Transfer to a food
processor and add the egg yolk, oil, raisins and
sugar. Whiz for a minute to combine. Add the
remaining ingredients and pulse to combine. Spoon
into the mini-muffin cases (about 1 tablespoon
for each mini muffin). Bake for 12–14 minutes,
until risen and firm to the touch.

Remove from the oven and allow to cool for
5 minutes, then transfer to a wire rack until cold.

Baked muffins are best stored frozen in an
airtight container or freezer bag. Defrost for
around 30 minutes at room temperature.

*These muffins are a great way to use up the odd
brown banana lurking in the bottom of the fruit
bowl. They are wonderful warm for breakfast or
for a teatime snack.*

Fresh fruit and peach melba dip

Put the raspberries, peach and icing sugar in a food processor and blend. Then press through a sieve to get rid of the seeds.

Mix the maple syrup with the yoghurt and stir in 2 tablespoons of the raspberry and peach purée. Serve with a selection of fruit.

🔪 5 MINUTES

🍴 3 PORTIONS

❄ SUITABLE FOR FREEZING

50 g (2 oz) raspberries, washed
1 ripe peach, stoned and chopped
about 1 tablespoon icing sugar, to sweeten
2 teaspoons maple syrup
50 g (2 oz) plain natural or Greek yoghurt
fresh fruit, such as apple, pear, banana, kiwi fruit, strawberries, mango, apricot, washed and cut into bite-size pieces, to serve

Fruit yoghurts and fromage frais can contain a lot of sugar, so it's best to buy plain varieties and sweeten them with fruit purées.

Yoghurt with fruit compote

/ 3 MINUTES

🔲 2 MINUTES

🦋 4–6 PORTIONS

❄ SUITABLE FOR FREEZING
(WITHOUT THE YOGHURT)

2 tablespoons apple juice
150 g (5 oz) blueberries,
   rinsed
2 tablespoons caster sugar
100 g (3½ oz) strawberries,
   washed, hulled and
   quartered
75 g (3 oz) raspberries,
   rinsed
plain natural or Greek
   yoghurt to serve

Put the apple juice and blueberries into a
saucepan. Gently heat until the blueberries just
start to soften (about 2 minutes). Remove from
the heat and add the caster sugar, strawberries
and raspberries. Stir until the sugar has dissolved.
Spoon into serving bowls and add the yoghurt.

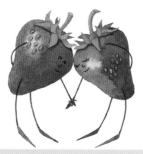

You could serve this delicious fruit compote with
porridge rather than yoghurt.

Cinnamon Scotch pancakes with banana and strawberries

To make the pancake batter, measure the baking powder, flour, sugar and cinnamon into a large mixing bowl. Add the eggs and milk, and whisk together until smooth.

Pour a little oil into the frying pan to coat the base and, when hot, spoon enough batter into the pan to just cover the bottom. Fry for 2 minutes on each side until lightly golden. Repeat until you have used all the batter, using a little more oil each time.

Serve with the banana and strawberries.

✏ 5 MINUTES
🍳 20 MINUTES
🕐 ABOUT 20 PANCAKES
❄ SUITABLE FOR FREEZING

1 teaspoon baking powder
225 g (8 oz) self-raising flour
50 g (2 oz) caster sugar
½ teaspoon ground
   cinnamon
2 eggs
250 ml (8 fl oz) milk
sunflower oil for frying
sliced banana and
   strawberries to serve

French toast with berries

🔪 2 MINUTES

🍳 5 MINUTES

🍪 8 TRIANGLES

❄ NOT SUITABLE FOR FREEZING

1 egg, beaten
1 tablespoon milk
2 teaspoons icing sugar,
   plus extra to serve
a good pinch of ground
   cinnamon
2 slices of bread, crusts
   removed
a knob of unsalted butter
raspberries and blueberries
   to serve

Mix together the egg, milk, icing sugar and cinnamon in a shallow bowl. Cut each slice of bread into triangles or, if you wish, use cookie cutters to make fun shapes. Dip the bread into the egg mixture, coating both sides.

Melt the butter in a frying pan, then fry the bread for about 5 minutes, turning halfway through, until golden brown and slightly fluffy.

Serve with the berries and a dusting of icing sugar and cinnamon.

Blueberries are rich in vitamin C and also contain betacarotene. The blue pigment anthocyanin in the skin helps protect us against cancer.

Quick rice pudding

🔪 10 MINUTES

🗔 30–35 MINUTES

🍴 6 PORTIONS

❄ SUITABLE FOR FREEZING

50 g (2 oz) pudding rice
600 ml (1 pint) milk
1–2 tablespoons caster sugar
½ teaspoon vanilla essence

Put all the ingredients in a heavy-bottomed saucepan. Bring to the boil, then reduce the heat, cover and simmer for 30–35 minutes, stirring occasionally. Mix with fruit, or one of the toppings suggested below.

Good things to serve with rice pudding:
- *stewed apple and pear*
- *tinned peaches*
- *chopped mango*
- *strawberry jam*
- *golden syrup*
- *fruit compote*

Strawberry and watermelon ice lollies

Put the sugar and water into a small saucepan and boil until syrupy (about 3 minutes). Allow to cool.

Purée the strawberries and press through a sieve to get rid of the seeds.

Purée the watermelon and mix with the puréed strawberries and cooled syrup. Pour the mixture into ice-lolly moulds and freeze.

🔪 5 MINUTES

🍳 3 MINUTES

🍥 6 SMALL LOLLIES

❄ SUITABLE FOR FREEZING

50 g (2 oz) caster sugar
60 ml (2 fl oz) water
250 g (9 oz) strawberries, washed and hulled
250 g (9 oz) watermelon, peeled, deseeded and cubed

Meal planner

	Day 1	Day 2	Day 3
Breakfast	**Fruity breakfast muesli** Milk	**Mini banana bran muffins** Fruit Yoghurt Milk	Scrambled egg Toast fingers Fruit Milk
Mid-morning	Milk	Milk	Milk
Lunch	**Tuna-melt toasty** Yoghurt	**Mini shepherd's pie** **Strawberry and watermelon ice lolly**	**Krispie fish fingers with lemon-mayo dip** Steamed broccoli and carrots Fruit
Mid-afternoon	Milk	Milk	Milk
Dinner	**Creamy chicken and basil pasta** Fruit	**Mashed sweet potato with spinach and cheese** Fruit	**Chicken and vegetable pie** Fromage frais
Bedtime	Milk	Milk	Milk

This meal planner is intended to be used as a guide. It's fine to give the same meal more than once in the same week. Give water or diluted fruit juice with lunch and dinner.

Day 4	Day 5	Day 6	Day 7
Porridge Fruit Yoghurt Milk	**French toast with berries** Milk	Ready Brek Fruit Yoghurt Milk	**Mini banana bran muffins** Cheese on toast Fruit Milk
Milk	Milk	Milk	Milk
Mini meatballs Steamed broccoli and carrots Fruit	**Fillet of fish with carrot, tomato and cheese sauce** **Quick rice pudding**	**Mini chicken balls** Steamed peas, carrots and broccoli Fruit	**Lamb, aubergine and sweet potato pie** **Strawberry and watermelon ice lolly**
Milk	Milk	Milk	Milk
Pasta risotto Yoghurt	**Bolognese with vegetables** Fruit	**Mashed potato and carrot with broccoli and cheese** Fruit	**Mini fish balls** Steamed broccoli and carrot Fruit
Milk	Milk	Milk	Milk

By nine months, your baby will probably be able to self-feed finger foods. Give toast, chunks of fruit and steamed or raw vegetables to supplement the meals suggested above.

Index